# MY NEW GRAMMY COUNTRY SONG LYRICS

Santiago Alexander "SANTI" Polito

**author**HOUSE®

*AuthorHouse™*
*1663 Liberty Drive*
*Bloomington, IN 47403*
*www.authorhouse.com*
*Phone: 833-262-8899*

*Published by AuthorHouse   03/26/2021*

*ISBN: 978-1-6655-2125-3 (sc)*
*ISBN: 978-1-6655-2124-6 (e)*

*Library of Congress Control Number: 2021906343*

*Print information available on the last page.*

# Genre Country Music

## "Name Of Song -
## Employee O Mine"

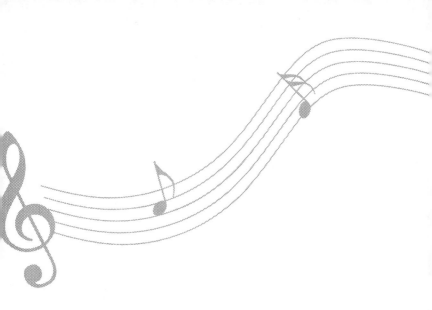

I wish you the best of luck in life

although you never had one with me.

When I saw your business

I learned that your environment drove your
business.

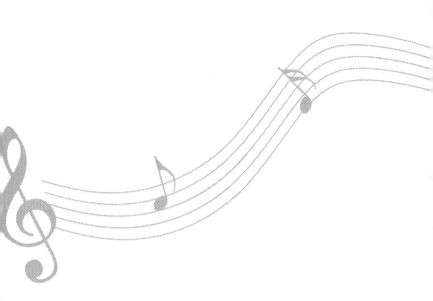

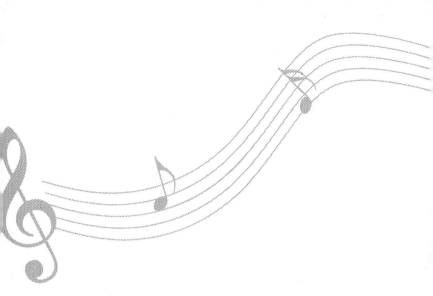

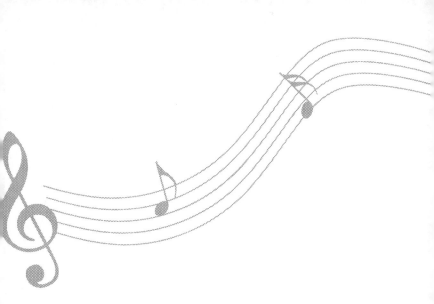

Although I just had to see you doing a certain thing

and that's when I learned to trust your luck

as well as your business instinct.

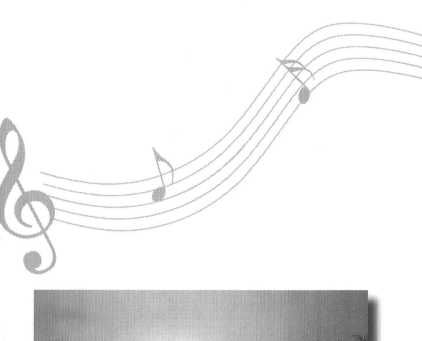

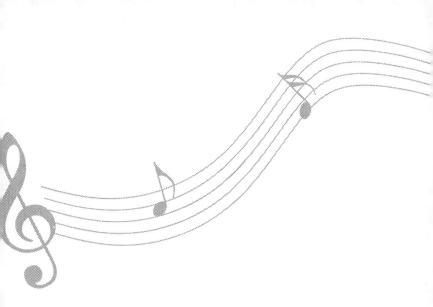

I learned from your luck and

that's something I'll never forget.

I found out one day that because of your luck

we'd have a better relationship.

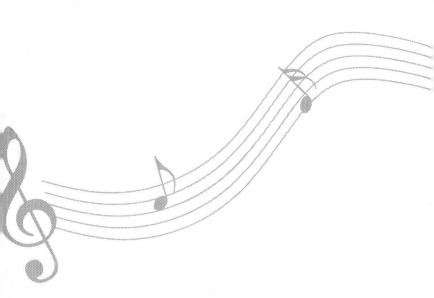

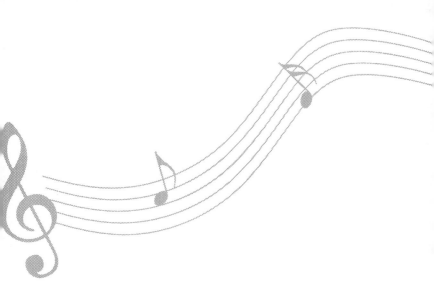

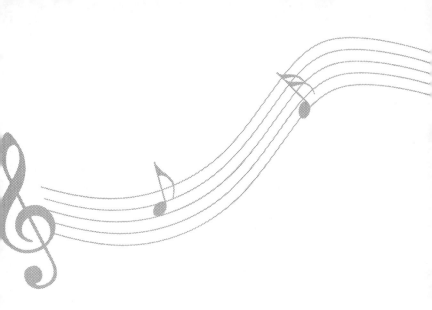

Your family asked me today

not to see you this year on your birthday.

Being the best employee and love of my life,

so I took your family's advice

not to see you this year for your special day.

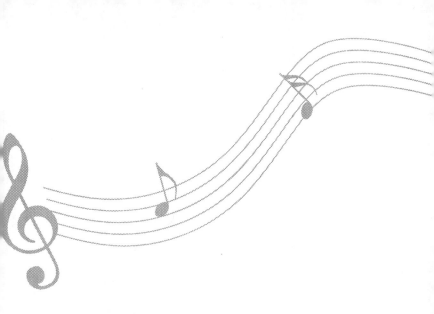

After that I started to see our love

unfurl into being a mom.

When I got to work that day,

my life as your employee,

you told me that I was

moving up at your place of business.

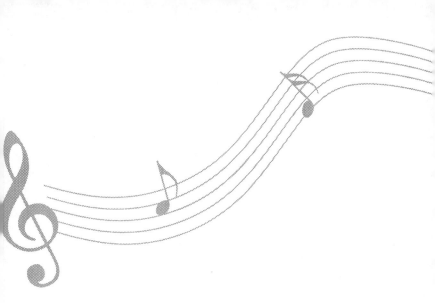

Pretty soon you'll be the one franchise.

Owner of the country. Long live Santiago.

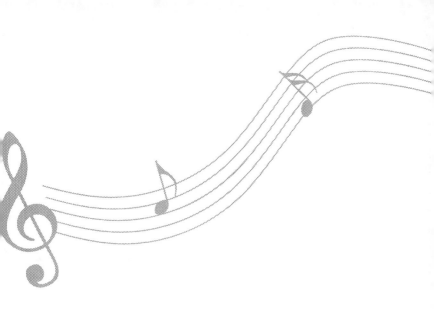

Later that same day I started thinking

about my franchise opportunity and
remembered your luck

and took to the bank.

Happy New Year and forth coming.

Printed in the United States
by Baker & Taylor Publisher Services